T0128827

BITTERSWEET
HONESTY

BITTERSWEET HONESTY

An Array of Inspiring Poetry

ISABELLA PATTON

BITTERSWEET HONESTY
AN ARRAY OF INSPIRING POETRY

iUniverse books may be ordered through booksellers or by contacting:

iUniverse
1663 Liberty Drive
Bloomington, IN 47403
www.iuniverse.com
1-800-Authors (1-800-288-4677)

Because of the dynamic nature of the Internet, any web addresses or links contained in this book may have changed since publication and may no longer be valid. The views expressed in this work are solely those of the author and do not necessarily reflect the views of the publisher, and the publisher hereby disclaims any responsibility for them.

Any people depicted in stock imagery provided by Thinkstock are models, and such images are being used for illustrative purposes only. Certain stock imagery © Thinkstock.

ISBN: 978-1-4917-9333-6 (sc)
ISBN: 978-1-4917-9334-3 (e)

Library of Congress Control Number: 2016907859

Print information available on the last page.

iUniverse rev. date: 10/18/2016

To my parents. Thank you for being the godly influence
I needed. I gained so much of which I cannot repay.

To my children, family, and close friends.

Additionally, to those close friends and family who helped
me through perilous times, listened to my poetry, and
offered invaluable encouragement and support, especially
those who not only read the entire book but even helped
me type the poetry. Thank you all for your generosity.

Most precious of all, thanks to God for giving me the thoughts,
words, and wisdom to write and carry out his purpose, to
whom I continue to pray for guidance and inspiration.

Contents

Introduction

Bittersweet Honesty is an anthology of poetry about the highs and lows of love, life, and even death. It is an expression of inner turmoil that somehow brings peace of mind. It is meant to reveal how in the midst of darkness, light can be seen, and because of the silence, one can hear the sweet noise of the world leading us to life.

Life is bittersweet.
Love is bittersweet.

Even death is bittersweet when one has faith in eternal life in Christ. The poetry doesn't always have the perfect pattern, because it is true to life. There are anomalies and events that have occurred in the poet's life that don't fit into perfect prose. However, most of the poems have a spiritual connotation that stems from the poet's morals, experiences, and—yes, dare I say—faith.

I believe that the highest degree of wisdom is found deep in the reflections of life. Like time heals, reflection clears and often reveals the bittersweet, honest details of hidden, painful, yet hopeful moments in the recesses of our minds. This is where poetry resides.

The Heart of a Poet

A poet's heart is a place to start.
It's where the soul begins to unfold.
You will find in many a kind
The better part is at the heart.

There is passion flowing from our minds.
It makes us vulnerable and exposed,
Like we're wearing Kick Me signs
Or literally sporting transparent clothes.

Life/Hope

A child.   A style.
A ray of hope.   A way of life.

Each takes its place and fills up the space.
Both child and style have a time and grow old.
Then are no more.

A child is born.   A style returns.

Both retake their place and fill the allotted space.

My First Love

I met my first love one day in September,
The most exciting time I can remember.
Ever so gently he touched my hand,
And a feeling came over me I couldn't understand.
He revealed himself in such a way
I knew in my heart close by me he'd stay.
As he reached out his hand and told me to take hold,
I yielded my body, mind, and soul.
Not a mere man, this lover of mine,
The epitome of perfection and so divine.
He is the one who calms my fears,
Restores my peace, and dries my tears.
And oh, yes, he is wealthy; he owns everything.
He is lord of lords and king of kings.
I would still love him if he only had dreams.

Marriage Is Work

I was filled with expectations of a love we would cherish.
I never imagined how with time it would perish.
The man that I married was not what I thought,
But at the time, he was all that I sought.
Now we both live in fear, I of him and him of me.
If he gives me an l, I'll go all the way to z.
I'm just afraid he'll make a fool out of me.
I open my mouth and speak my mind,
But he doesn't listen most of the time.
Sometimes I get weary and go to God all teary.
He consoles me, and I begin to feel cheery.
I often wonder how long must I toil.
We are so different, like water and oil.
I don't give up though, in spite of it all.
I hear in God's word, long suffering's the call.
Some may wonder how one can endure
The heartbreak, insecurities, feeling unloved, I am sure.
Well, Jesus, my refuge in times of despair,
Renews me, and all of my burdens he bears.
These days, one can often escape in a hurry.
Just get a divorce, start over—no worry.
But that's not the answer for me though, you see.
True to God, to Jesus, to His Word, I must be.
In all this, I'm thinking there is something I'm missing.
A husband's a joy, a thrill to be kissing!

Life

Unlike most, I don't want much—
Just love, security so real I can touch,
To spend the day having fun in the sun.
Relax. Slow down. Why stay on the run?

Spend time with a friend.
Take a jog around the bend.
See the world every minute.
Use everything in it.

The flowers, the mountains, oceans, and trees.
Blue skies, birds singing, frog, crickets, and leaves.
Live life; it's for living, and death is for dying.
I believe on the other side in heaven is no crying.

You know one day this will all come to an end.
Life, death, and then eternity begins.
And when you look back over all that you've done,
Did you take the time to receive God's Son?

Or were you a wealthy, famous lost one?

A Dear Friend

There is someone I call a friend,
As close as a family member or kin.
Sometime I'm confused and unclear within
As to where my friend ends and where I begin.

As I reflect back to how our friendship started,
I wonder if we will ever somehow be parted.
We've endured pain, heartbreak, and sorrows together,
Helping one another our storms to weather.

Though it just happened, it was not our aim.
We've shared degrading humiliation and shame,
But armored with Christ, our weapons were formed.
With him we were strong and weathered the storms.

Respect–Honor–Love

Crossing the street as cars swish by
Is a little old lady about five feet high.
Help her across. Don't push or shove her.
Show some respect. She's a loving mother.

Sitting on a park bench, reading the word,
Stopping for a moment and feeding the birds.
Walk over, smile, extend him your hand.
In WWII, he fought for this land.

A great man of God, nobody's worked harder.
I proudly proclaim to you that man is my father.
A woman who helped you your goals to reach,
None other than Mother, her wisdom to teach.

Children of God, both great and small,
Don't be misled. Listen to the call.
Honor thy father and thy mother,
And for Christ sake, love ye one another.

Waiting Room

I was sitting in a waiting room, crunching on Cheerios.
It was quiet—no radios, TVs, or stereos.
I paid the co-pay and hurriedly sat down.
Then I relaxed until my chart could be found.

The nurse called my name at the corridor door.
She checked my weight and blood pressure once more.
I waited in the examining room, listing my problems.
Profoundly I knew that only God could solve them.

Doctors are knowledgeable in their areas of expertise,
Minor sickness health issues, even chronic diseases.
But I realize that some ailments run deeper—
Lack of finances, faith, forgiving hearts to speak of.

Some things a doctor can't see on an x-ray.
Even though they look hard, try as they may,
They can't see the softness or hardness of the heart,
And they haven't a clue as to where the soul starts.

We African Americans

We African American people,
We've been through so much and have come a long way.
And as we look back, we can marvel at today.
Our ancestors fought long and hard for this life,
And their time expired before using these rights.
We are the recipients of the fruits of their labor.
Because of their prayers, we've received God's favor.
We have gained so much to hold and cherish.
For these they suffered, and many of them perished.
Our plight is not over; racism still exists.
We must all do our part to rid ourselves of this.
How do we do it? Through prayer, truth, and love,
Keeping our eyes stayed on God above.
The Bible says perfect love casts out all fear,
And God will console us and dry all our tears.
So as we endure life's trials and tribulations,
All praises to God, who strengthens our nation.
Not by power nor might we have come to this place.
Our God will not leave us; we will finish this race.

Children

At conception, children are empty buckets.
As they grow, they begin to fill up.
If you put in love, you get great results.
Put in hate for a poor fate.
Be careful of what they eat or drink,
And be very watchful of how they think.
Compassion and discipline are what they need.
Neglect them, and you will be sorry indeed.
Teach honesty, humility, and self-control.
Observe them as their lives begin to unfold,
Daughters grow into their mother's roles.
Sons that are truly a joy to behold.

The Good Old Days

Back in the day when boys came a courting,
They'd come appropriate and not just sportin',
With thoughts first of marriage,
Before the baby carriage.
Humbly, respectfully, and never grumbly,
Sat on the couch
As Mom and Dad moved about.
No kissing or touching. There was no rushing.
And for Christ sake, no sex. That was clearly a vex.
There were some liberties like glances and smiles
When Mom and Dad agreed holding hands was allowed.
For Rachel, Jacob worked seven years long,
And then even more his love was so strong.
Sacrifices like that don't happen today.
Nowadays, women are just given away.
Then after the wedding, things change dramatically,
And discontentment replaces love ecstatically.
Women are workaholics while men run amuck.
Children roam the streets trying to earn a couple of bucks.
The entire home is empty and unkempt.
When was the last time the floors got swept?
Well, don't ask the woman.
She is busy earning money.
And talk to the hand
Because men don't understand.

A Purpose-Driven Teacher

This is a poem I just can't get going.
I'm working on the rhymes, but it's just not flowing.
There's a dream that I dreamed but have not yet reached.
Thinking on it, praying on it, to God I beseech.

Now I am commissioned by God to teach
Children to critically think and speak.
They come to me downhearted and trodden.
Places from which some of them come are just rotten.

Some seem happy, but some have the blues.
Some have been mentally or physically abused.
I give it my all, for I know it's God's will,
But many are behind with diminishing skills.

Though teaching, I love and want only to stay.
Other responsibilities keep pulling me away.
While we focus on testing and scores of our state,
What about the children? What about their fate?

Our children are missing out on basic needs,
Largely due to rhetoric and political greed.
Get on the bandwagon and fight for their rights.
Each of them should have a productive life.

A Grave Race

There is a race that is going on,
A rocky road with lots of stones.
It's like a test that seals your fate,
So start on time and don't be late.
It is a race to the pearly gate.
My older brother, Melvin, beat me there.
My heart cried out, "It isn't fair."
Then went two more of my father's sons.
But I must wait; it's not my turn.
Eventually, my time will come.
This race is different from all the rest.
To make the grave and past the test,
It's not first place you must achieve
But whom you know and what you believe.
Please beware; don't be deceived.
We do not war against human beings
But principalities and things unseen.
'Tis sad that some won't make it though,
For they will choose to follow foe.
But I will hold firm to the God I know.
If you listen and obey,
"Well done," you'll hear the father say.
It not who's fast or how you play.
Stay on the path and go the right way.

Go with God

God will not send us unprepared.
He'll tell us when and what to share.
As we study to show ourselves approved,
We'll be available and ready to be used.

The way is clear. The spirit will show.
Be armed for battle and ready to go.
No need to worry about what to say.
Jesus is the life, truth, and the way.

If you haven't invited Christ into your heart,
Then this is where you need to start.
He paved the way and gave the sample;
Now we must follow his example.

Suffering

To suffer long, one must be strong.
A sacrifice for the sake of Christ.
A cross to bear, a love to share.
This love of God spreads everywhere.
To give as much as Jesus gave—
Not only gave, but Jesus saves.
I heard the call so long ago.
I hesitated and let him know
I am unworthy, unfit to live.
And what if flesh won't let me give?
I'm not as strong as some might think.
Instead of swimming, I just might sink.
But then he spoke his words so plain.
"I'll be your strength, so do not strain."
"Why suffer long?" I asked the Lord,
Already wrinkled, scarred, and soiled.
"So often, Lord, I tire and fail.
I feel weak and very frail.
If I can do all things through Christ
Why don't I always win the fight?
And though I know you're in control,
I'm stilled uncomforted and consoled.
I know the failure is within me.
Help me, Father, your way to be."

Was Meant to Be

I wanted to be first to drive the tractor.
I also dreamed of being an actor.
Neither of these happened for me.
It simply was not meant to be.

When things don't go the way I plan,
I'm puzzled. I do not understand.
I wasn't first to drive the tractor,
No chance at all of being an actor.

I know now that there was no need
To do these things, just to succeed.
I had to find and fulfill my purpose,
One much deeper than on the surface.

There was a call beyond my desire,
One to teach, to love and inspire.
I now feel joy and complete
Because this is what was meant to be.

What Christ Would Do

What Christ would do is known to the elite few.
The carnal-minded man cannot know God's plans.

He draws near to us as we draw near to him.
His mercy and grace he gives the least of them.

Because he's my savior, I am privileged to hope,
And in his strength, I'm empowered to cope.

As he moves in my life, I can see the results.
I know in his word I can totally trust.

While I sojourn this world, his blood covers me.
Things I never saw I am quickened to see.

The Holy Spirit leads me, comfort and guide.
His unconditional love is where I hide.

Thank you, Lord God, for taking me in,
And while I was yet a sinner, redeeming my sins.

King Nebuchadnezzar

King Nebuchadnezzar needed spiritual insight;
He on his own could not see the light.

Not one of his wise men the truth could reveal,
Those things that God alone could unseal.

When Daniel went in and desired of the king,
Asking for time to seek God on his dream,

He was granted his request, and Daniel through prayer
Saw the king's future and how he would fare.

Though somewhat amazingly, Daniel foretold
Of events to come and how they would unfold.

The king, though he listened, he did not yield.
And so as an animal, he ate in the field.

Often we choose to follow the path of sin.
We follow it right to a terrible end.

And though we are warned from our wickedness to turn,
We rather sometimes take the hard way to learn.

Lord, What Would You Have Me Do?

Down on one knee, seeking you,
Make clear to me what you want me to do.
Boldly I come and with a plea,
Magnetically draw me to thee.

With praises, Lord, I lift you high,
Remembering your Word, but if I, if I …
I believe that if you are lifted up from the earth,
We'd all be better off, not worse.

Lord, I've been in your care for a very long time.
Your love, your grace, your mercy are mine.
When I sought you, you found me.
You gave me peace. You set me free.

The Holy Spirit now lives inside,
And under the blood is where I hide.
How do I say it, or how can I stress?
In your care, I'm with the best.

I have tasted and know, Lord, that you're good.
Who? What can compare to you?
Nothing.
No one could.

Seeking

What is measurable in this field?
Knowing Christ and doing his will.

Is it possible we can tell
When the work of Christ is well?

Is it when we go to church?
Get on our knees and pray and such.

Or better still live in his will?
Obey commandments like do not kill.

Or maybe we must do it all
In order to answer Jesus's call.

Whatever the spirit says to you,
That is what God wants you to do.

A Seeker's Review

Lord, do you remember the time
I sat by the window at early dawn?
I called out to you again and again.
I wonder if you think back to when
I asked you to put a star in the sky.
I sat by the window, and, Lord, did I cry.
I almost gave up then, by and by.
You took my hand and directed my sight.
I almost couldn't believe my eyes
But realized it was no surprise,
Because nothing is too hard for you.

And who was that standing at the foot of my bed,
Watching me, stalking me? And I wasn't afraid.
Why did my eyes suddenly open that night?
Really, who was it? And why wasn't I affright?
Was it an angel watching over me that night?
Or a demonic presence to destroy my life?
Is there a revelation I have not yet found?
A destiny for me that might the world astound?
Another time when lightning struck,
I felt it hit my lips and stuck.
And what about the vision of the woman and man?
Outside the window they did stand.
Remember how fear just took control
And paralyzed my body mind and soul?
I never understood it, Lord.

Was I supposed to prophesy?
I was only a child. What did I know?
I told her, Lord, but did she believe
Or think it was just a bad dream?
If it was real, I hope she took heed.

A Mother's Prayer

A mother knelt down to pray one night.
'Twas cool and quiet as she turned out the light.
She talked with her father about all of her problems,
Seeking his advice as to how to solve them.

She prayed for her children, each one by name,
And asked God to bless them all the same.
She mentioned her husband, ever so kind,
Praying he would stay in the right frame of mind.

Asking wisdom for her and wisdom for him,
And oneness of heart for both of them.
Now listen, all, and remember Mother's prayer,
For it is sincere and flooded with care.

Soothing Thoughts

My mind is adrift with drizzling thoughts—
Some happy, some sad, and some matter not.
Sing a song full of woes to console a sad mind,
And lyrics so cheerful soothe all other kinds.

Music, I believe, is medicine to the soul.
Anyone can relate to it, no matter how old.
A shepherd looked up and heard music in the air.
As the song says, I'm certain there is a heaven up there.

I believe I will get there and join that choir.
I'll sing for eternity and never tire.
All praises to God on high, lift his name—
Our Lord, our Savior, Redeemer proclaim.

A Storm

A storm arose in the cool of the day.
I was tossed to and fro and blown far away.

Landing on a rooftop adrift in a flood,
Birds flying through the air sang up above.

Sitting on the housetop, staring at the sight,
Praying to be rescued from the fearful height.

Alone and afraid as night came to call,
I dozed and dreamed I had begun to fall.

Then Jesus, with outstretched arms, reached out
And saved me with a mighty shout.

He took me out of darkness tossed;
It was his choice by way of the cross.

Redeemed that I am from all of my faults,
Christ Jesus now my eternal boss.

Salvation

I'm listening to a message that says I am completed.
From the book of life, my name cannot be deleted.

A world of sin and shame I can leave.
All is forgiven, and Christ I receive.

Reach out touch and take what God has given.
All through his son, and he is risen.

My father owns all—both houses and land,
Everything made by the work of his hand.

Both joy and tribulations, he is master of it all.
He transformed Saul and made him Paul.

What I can do? Nothing, I confess.
On Jesus's power I can truly rest.

Choose this day. Whom will you serve?
Follow the straight path or take the crooked curve.

Young People Today

The world is going crazy in a spooky way.
The music sounds scary that the children play.
While looking straight ahead, you better watch your back.
You don't know what they're packing, baby; that's a fact.

In the good ole days when I was much younger,
I dreamed about the future, and I would often wonder
Where my life would take me and in what direction.
I wanted to be famous and to reach perfection.

You know that didn't happen because I'm a loner.
And how can one be famous as a one and only?
Soon I learned perfection was an empty dream,
For one could never get there as a human being.

When you try your best, you still don't pass the test.
After all of that, you're still a filthy mess.
So try to live for Jesus and just do your best.
Try to be obedient, and you'll be blessed.

Insanity/Burnout

In this state of mind, I could go insane
And not even know how to come in from the rain.

The pressure is coming on, and I can't deal.
I can't even explain just how I feel.

Without a reason, I'm sluggish and tired.
If I go to work like this, I could be fired.

I feel so full I could just explode.
This weight that I'm carrying, it's a heavy load.

I get home from work, and I'm all worn out.
Keep a safe distance, or I just might shout.

A Ghostly Presence

A noise at the door.
Then a ghostly frame
Appeared at the hallway
And toward me came.
For a while, I was frozen
In place by fear.
As she floated down the corridor,
I could see she was sheer.
Then horror overtook me,
And courage forsook me.
I didn't have the power
To move or run.
She didn't seem to care
Or show any concern.

Submission

Submission is a mysterious thing
When bound by a wedding ring,
Rendering all of one's earthly deeds
To serve and yield to another's needs.

Not fully aware of what it means
To follow the heart, to achieve a dream,
That which we seek is not what we find.
We often want our lives to rewind.
You've heard the saying "Love is blind."

Still,

We must show Christ's love to our brothers,
Submitting one to one another.
This do in reverence to Jesus Christ.
The word of God says this is right.
We must obey with all our might.
He is the way, truth, and the light.

Mother's Touch

It's icy cold in this waiting room,
Not at all like home.
Home is warm. We'll be there soon,
In a more pleasant zone.
I don't know why it's taking so long.

I know that God is in control,
But fear has gripped my very soul.
Please, God, my mother's hand you hold.
Help me remember that you console.

My mother is so very special.
Even to you she is so precious.
May we please have her here longer?
I want to see her vital and stronger.

I do remember what Jesus said.
Not my will but thine be done.
As she lies in her hospital bed,
I have faith the battle you've won.

Now, Mommy dearest, best of all,
Hear the savior as he calls.
Yes, he's tugging at your heart.
I am the one he gave a start.

He made me aware of just how much
I love you and long to have your touch.

Help

A hand out for a hand up
Will free our people
From a bitter cup.
A rising flight
To a rising star.
Remind us of who
And what we are.
The mystery
Of human life.
The unity
Of man and wife.
All have a place in society,
The great and vast variety.

A Live House

I had a house all furnished and new.
This house was alive; it even grew.
And though it was furnished, it was empty within,
Because its rooms were filled with sin.

This caused the building to weaken and fall.
It shook the foundation and shattered the walls.
Then came a guest from heaven to visit,
This person a Paraclete, advocate, spirit.

He immediately started to work on the house.
When he was finished, there wasn't even a mouse.
He started repairing from top to bottom,
And finally there was nothing left broken or rotten.

Surrender

Oh, heavenly Father, take control
Of my body, mind, and soul.
Cause me only to do your will.
Tell my flesh, "Peace. Be still."

My desire is obedient to be
Quite frequent and expediently
It's your blessings that I seek;
Otherwise, havoc I may wreak.

When you call, I will answer,
For my soul you have ransomed.
I can't do this in my flesh.
I've already failed the test.

Now I ask for your assistance.
Remove temptation and resistance.

Your Will, Lord

I asked the Lord to give me guidance.
I needed to know which way to turn.
I needed his help in making decisions.
I felt so anxious I couldn't discern.

So often when we seek God on a subject,
We want him to do whatever we please.
But he doesn't always give what we want;
He looks deeper and fulfills our needs.

We are sometimes left feeling disappointed,
Disheartened, angry, and betrayed.
We forget that we gave him the authority
To show the way when we prayed.

Daddy, I Know ...

The years and time consumed your mind,
But I believe your spirit is still around.
Let your spirit linger near
Long enough these words to hear.
Daddy, I know what you were trying to do,
And I want you to know that I agree with you.
You put up a fight, tried to teach us right.
I love and respect you to the highest height.
I remember waking up before daylight in the morning.
The roosters crowing was our first warning.
You yielded your strength into farming the land.
For God and family, Daddy, you took a stand.
Not only family, you reached out to the community.
I know that your purpose was to instill unity.
If it didn't work, Daddy, you did your part.
Others may have wanted to but didn't know where to start.
They say the old way is a thing of the past,
But you taught us that what we do for Christ lasts.
Daddy, those points that you couldn't get through,
If God shows me how, I'll carry on for you.
Because, Daddy, I know what you were trying to do,
And I want you to know that I agree with you.

Dying Alive

Don't be nice to me because I'm dying.
What if God should change his mind
And decide to keep me around
For a really long time?
Would you be upset if I didn't die?
Make you wanna break down and cry?
Wouldn't it irk your nerves to know
It was a trick and I didn't go?
Have a eulogy for the living.
Tell how I am loving and giving.
Absolutely give me flowers
And sit and talk with me for hours.
There will be no need for tears,
And perfect love casts out all fears.
I've got something I must tell you.
Pass it on to others too.
I have acquired eternal life
By accepting God's son, Jesus Christ.
Even when my flesh shall perish,
You can still life memories cherish.
The grave
Is not where my life ends
But immortality begins.

Victims of Katrina (2005)

We've suffered losses throughout this year.
Many lost loved ones, toils, and fears.
This storm brought troubles to our hearts.
We've had to stop, evaluate, and restart.

Some lost everything they had,
While others grieved loved ones and were very sad.
But while we suffer, Jesus is teaching,
Many a souls pursuing and reaching.

What was the purpose? Why did we go through?
The answer lies between God and you.
No one else knows your plight;
Only God can show you the light.

911 Jesus

911 Jesus for salvation.

911 Jesus for conversation.

911 Jesus for inspiration.

911 Jesus for innovation.

911 Jesus for renewing.

911 Jesus for self-reviewing.

911 Jesus for cleansing from sinning.

911 Jesus for new beginning.

911 Jesus on knees bending.

911 Jesus when life is ending.

Fiftieth Anniversary

What's in a marriage of fifty years?
What in a lifetime of joys and tears?
You both have wisdom that exceeds your days.
You are an inspiration in all your ways.

Your hearts of gold, gentle yet strong.
You instill confidence; you don't lead wrong.
Many marriages crumble under pressure,
Never taking time to savor their treasure.

But in your commitment, you held to your love.
The adversary tried, but you are covered by the blood.
Though you have gone through diverse situations,
God was victorious through those complications.

Marriage is a journey, so continue in strength.
God is still with you, though years you have spent.
This much I know and confidently say;
If he brought you this far, he'll go all the way.

A Love like Yours

Can't quite explain it; it's like no other.
More like a mystery I can't uncover.
A yearning within I must discover.
I got on the telephone and asked my mother,
But then something struck me and sent my heart reeling.
Maybe it's not me you want; it's just that feeling.
I want you, I need you, but you're just not willing.
Now I can see that you're not so appealing.
It's time for me to move on and anew start living.
A love like yours maybe just isn't love,
And I've got to look higher through the stars above.
To get what I need and to live my dreams,
I can't get from you, or so it seems.
You haven't got the passion, and you haven't got the means
To satisfy my hunger and my bell to ring.
You were right about one thing: yes, I was afraid,
Afraid of losing you, my twenty-eight-year fix,
Of having no one here to kick it with.
I'm over it now; I can move on.
No time to dwell on how I've been wronged.
Life is precious, and time is short,
And you can't have my dreams to thwart.
We have been blessed in the life that we've shared,
So I love you, and you will always be in my prayers.

Join Forces

Lord, this project is too big for me alone,
So let's do something with it together.

I want to help the students become inspired.
Please, join me in this endeavor.

If you undergird me, we can do great things.
So be the wind beneath my wings.

Though it's not clear, the vision is here.
Loose my passion and harness my fears.

Everything in its proper place,
Allow me to fill the empty space.

Use me; help me get through to the children.
Show me how to help them make good decisions.

The choices they make will decide their fate.
I want to steer them away from mistakes.

Song

Lord, I know you have a plan,
But I sure don't understand.
My ways are higher than your ways.
I am the ancient of days.

Lord, it's hard to conceive;
Your love is so good indeed.
My child, I'm right by your side,
And all your needs I'll supply.

(Chorus) See, every breath that you take,
It is a blessing from me.
And every step that you make,
It's grace and mercy, you see.
If truly you abide in me and my word abides in you,
Ask what you will, and that is just what I'll give.
You must remember my child:
I am real.

Lord, I want to be strong.
I need your help to hold on.
My child, I'll give you my strength.
I'll never leave you alone.

(Repeat chorus.)

Memories Revisited

For Thanksgiving (2007), I visited my mom and dad.
As I began to reminisce, I felt a little sad.
Some loved ones I had known and who were long since gone
Came back to me, and it was oh so strong.
My aunt and uncle used to sit on their porch.
Thoughts of Grandpa and my brothers
Made the tears flow more.
Each loved one that left me took a piece of my soul,
And I am left with a fraction of the old.
Now more recently, my daddy has gone.
I am sitting here feeling so alone.
Although he has died, his presence is felt.
It almost feels like he never left.
My mother is still with us, and that is a blessing.
Through all of the losses, we've learned tough lessons.
Now we must hold firm to what we have.
Live, learn, and love and share.

Regrets

We have been redeemed from the enemy's hand,
And the time has come for us to take a stand.
So often we feel, but we never put in words.
If we don't speak, it will never be heard.
If we don't attempt to somehow show,
How will our loved ones ever know?
As journeys end and new ones begin,
We have lost and gained new friends.
Some will find that we've missed so much.
We'll have regrets about those we didn't touch.
Many sons and fathers departing at odds,
Grandfathers trying their problems to solve.
Daughters love mothers, but they didn't tell,
Even when the Holy Spirit within compelled.
As she blows her last breath, they sat by her bed,
Desperately wishing to her they had said,
"Mama, I love you. Please don't go,
For if you do, I'll miss you so."

The Dark Side of Love

The dark side of love,
Even that comes from above.
What's the order of seduction?
Where can we find formal instruction?
Emotions spring forth in explosions.
Sensuality gleans mental poetry.

So much passion, so much fire.
Chemistry, ecstasy it inspires.
Though the mouth speaks true lies.
Through the heart honesty drives.
When we were young, we had a crush.
Oh, but true love—what a rush.

When you give someone your heart,
Yield to him your better part.
From him you have expectations:
Loyalty, love, and dedication.
In your love, you want to trust,
But mostly what you do is fuss.

Sometimes men want mind control.
They grow bitter and so cold.
Money has a role to play.
Loss of a marriage, price to pay.
How can we our love perceive
When we're so easily deceived?

Perhaps if we would take our time,
We would cease to be so blind.
We might sense when love is real.
The truth of love, time may reveal.
It is much more than what we feel.

Dynamic Daughters

JESSICA

Well, what can I say? She is wise beyond her years.
She is the one who consoles when there are tears.
She protests, wonders, and thinks too hard,
Oblivious of the fact that she's holding the cards.
If beauty was a crime, she would have to do time.
Smart, versatile, and has a great mind.
Gifted and courageous, she strengthens her peers.
I have seen God using her down through the years.
As she ages, I fear that she might stray.
There is time when she ventures toward a worldly way.

MEILLETTIS

High-strung and flighty, full of shape and style.
A glow all around her and a sensational smile.
Upon entering a room, she instantly draws a crowd.
From whence cometh her help, she looks to the sky.
She's a rising star, a diamond though uncut,
Some of her edges sharp to the touch.
She's a warrior of sort but a tender heart.
She nurses sick animals and repairs their broken parts.
To know her is to love her. She's fun to be with.
Her true friends stay close; on her, they won't quit.
Though empowered by God, confidence she lacks.
If only she knew the power she packs.

JAQUNDA

The eldest is eccentric and exceptionally bright.
Tall, strong frame, with amazing insight.
She is wise, sets goals, and excels in her task,
Unselfishly helping most anyone who asks.
She won't back down. She speaks her mind.
A force to be reckoned with. In her, you will find
A rare beauty. She shines like gold.
These are the signs that God is in control.
Not to be toyed with, her rights she knows.
Angels seem to guide her wherever she goes.

My Son-Shine, Deion

He came to us a little late,
Through a niece, but still we knew it was fate.
A blessing in disguise, no doubt.
Only God knew how it would all turn out.
A son we never had before.
With God, we boldly walked through that door,
Like unchartered territory or land unfarmed.
Reluctantly, he agreed to let me be his mom.
He peered through the door, a bewildered face.
I feared we might be invading his space.
He ran to a chair in the foster home and sat down.
From the corner of his eyes, he looked on with a frown.
I sensed his discomfort at strangers so near,
So I gave him time to overcome his fears.
Then slowly but surely, he ventured close.
We played and sang songs until I had to go.
Our first visit was short; we stayed only a little while.
But before I left him, he gave me a smile. Wow!
Now I don't know all the ins and outs,
But Gods know what this is all about.
We didn't plan this, had no way of knowing,
And he didn't even come from our loins.
But one thing is for sure, and I know that it's true:
I love him as much as the others,
I do.

I'm Always Here

I have been watching over you for quite some time.
You've grown older now, but you're each still mine.

I have seen you all changing over the years,
From infants, toddlers, and teens with great fears.

As you ventured through adolescence and into adulthood,
You seemed to feel you were misunderstood.

You put up walls. Behind pride you hide.
And you don't seem to notice that I am always on your side.

I am beginning to realize that I must let you go.
I don't know how to because I love you so.

How does one part with her children so dear,
When I have kept watch for so many years?
For you, I am always here.

From Pain to Peace

Although you've moved away from me,
I can't escape my love for thee.
I fear the hurt I carry
Is far too great for me.
I thought that if you had to choose,
Your first choice would be me.
Somehow, you weren't wise enough,
How deep my love to see.
If I could climb the tallest tree
And hide between the leaves,
How safe I'd be away up there,
To hide the hurt from me.
I cannot utter words so clear,
The pain I feel so deep.
But if I stay way out of sight,
No one would see but me.
Oh, God, I can't go on this way.
Lord Jesus, rescue me.
I'm broken, humbled, tattered, and torn.
Oh how I long for thee
To save my heart from agony.
From bondage, set me free.
If this is your will and meant to be,
Then give your peace to me.

The Client

Walked into my office boldly,
Proclaiming to me and very coldly.
"I will not talk to you," he said.
"You will not know what's in my head.
I cannot stand you counselor types,
And you don't know what I am like.
I talk to my friends; they understand.
They cry with me and hold my hands.
I've lots of problems I won't tell.
The life I live is living hell.
I have done drugs. Sometimes I smoke.
Though not at school, I've tried some coke.
When I'm at home, my parents are mean.
I do it all. I cook and clean.
My old man is never home.
My mom is lonely, so I'm alone.
I come to school to get relief,
And then the teachers give me grief.
So what's a kid like me to do?
Confused and hurt, can you rescue?
So, yes, you talk a real good game,
But you don't know from whence I came.
My people don't talk to me like you.
They yell, they curse, and beat me too.

No words to encourage me to do what's right.
Their best advice: get out of my sight."

Yeah Right

If I tell you about my life,
You will probably say, "Yeah right."
About rising before daylight,
Feeling that it wasn't right.
If I tell you I picked cotton,
Gathered eggs from the hen house, rotten.
If I tell you about my fright,
Seeing ghosts in the middle of the night,
You will probably say, "Yeah right."
If I tell you about my dreams
And horrific things I've seen,
If I tell you about my tears,
How they mysteriously disappeared,
You will say I made it up.
You will probably say, "Yeah right."
If I tell you about my faith,
About Jesus's saving grace.
He was crucified, died, and then
How he cleansed me from my sin.
If you don't know him like I do,
You will think that I'm cuckoo.
You will think it's just a hoax.
You will say I'm full of smoke.

And you'll probably say, "Yeah right."

Love Woes

Having been so hurt, I was numb to love.
But in my dream, love came to me.
He touched my hand, and an electric shock
Went to my heart, and I got a jumpstart.
Adrenalin of passion started to flow.
I thought, *why now?*
I am not too old for love.
And for me, the world is too cold for love.
I don't even have enough life to love.
Too many years spent to be able to hold onto love.
Do I even have the strength to fight for love?
Though lonely, do I have a right to love?
In my youth, I gave my heart and soul to love.
The mistake was in who I chose to love.
Now I haven't much faith in love.
Love is fleeting; one may not stay in love.

Are You Sure We Were Poor?

My sister said that we were poor.
I didn't know.
I thought we had it all.
Held my head high, I stood tall.
Can't remember ever being hungry.
So much family, we weren't lonely.
Mother and father and food to share.
Brothers and sisters, enough to spare.
The trees, the vines, the crops, and more.
How could I know we were poor?
I didn't know.
Shucks, we had our own smoke house,
More than enough for human and mouse.
If we were poor, I sure didn't know,
But my older sister said we were poor.
Right off the trees, we could pick fresh cherries.
On the way to school, we picked blackberries.
When I say fresh, I mean right off the vine.
It was their season; they were sweet all the time.
Like I said, I really didn't know
But my older sister said we were poor.
Our garden was full of collard greens,
And we were forever shelling beans.
In January, we slaughtered hogs.
We fed them corn right off the cobs,
Peanuts, peas, potatoes, melons.
Some rotted before we could eat or sell 'em.
Cotton, cucumbers by the pound,
As much or as many as could be found.
Tomatoes, okra, onion, garlic, and chives,
Enough to keep us all our lives.
So much more than I can tell,
But my sister said it,
So oh well.

You Could Have Chosen Life

You were a mother, daughter, wife.
You didn't have to go that way.
You could have chosen life.
You could at least have tried to stay
And faced your problems anyway.
You taught others to make right choices.
Your action contradicted your own voice.
Of course it's hard; sometimes we fall.
But don't lose hope; on Jesus call.
His mercy endures forever on all.
All you had to do was ask.
He would have helped you face the task.
You don't walk this road alone.
God forgives when we go wrong.
If you give to him your heart,
Submit to him your better part,
He will tell you what to do.
Faithfully he'll see you through.
You didn't have to end in strife.
You can live. Why not choose life?
You should have chosen life.

Listen

The hearts and minds of the children speak,
Saying
My needs aren't met, so I am incomplete.
You're telling me I must do things your way,
But how can I when I am not okay?
My dad walked out on us, and Mama needs help.
I have no choice; this I must accept.
He's got a family on the other side of town,
Takes care of them but doesn't want us around.
Doesn't come to visit or pay child support.
Only God knows why Mama won't take him to court.
She works two jobs and can't pay all the bills.
I'm still in school, and I've got no skills.
They are to blame, but we kids take the fall.
Nobody seems to care about us at all.
My friends tell me they will be the family I need.
We can get money if we sell this weed.
Meanwhile, the police are laying in wait.
They have no mercy; they are filled with hate.
I feel helpless. My life is a mess.
Who can help me? How can I be blessed?
Still
The hearts and minds of the children speak.
Influential ears, they are trying to reach.
Anyone who cares about their plight,
Willing and able to join the fight.
If you are commissioned to answer the call,
Don't let this on deaf ears fall.
While
We go to church and fill the pews,
The collection plate comes, and we pay dues.
Children in our communities live with neglect.
No one reaches out when their needs aren't met.

Daddy's Laugh

When Daddy laughs, a flower blooms.
Winter flows into early June.
Daddy laughed.
When Daddy laughs, I feel okay.
I know that things will go my way.
Daddy laughed.
Daddy smiled.
When Daddy smiles, the sun will rise,
And my sisters and I will see blue skies.
Daddy smiled.
If Daddy cries,
I see the truth in Daddy's eyes.
Honest, sincere, he is the prize.
I also cry if Daddy cries.
Daddy's heart.
Daddy's heart is made of gold,
The strength of which cannot be told.
Daddy's love.
For Daddy's love, there are no words … no words …

These Tears

These tears I weep, I weep for me.
I do not weep these tears for thee.
I weep because I miss you so,
The times we spent, the places we'd go.

These tears I cry are for the fun,
Laughter, and hanging in the sun.
These tears are because I think of you,
Spending time talking with you too.

These tears I cry are not for thee.
I heartily weep but for me,
For unconditional love and friendship,
Closer than one's own kinship.

These tears I cry are for the years,
For the bittersweet, honest tears.
I weep for times when love was strong,
When we struggled, but we held on.

During those times, we were together,
Clinging to each other, whatever the weather,
When life was hard and troubles long,
And when we thought we couldn't go on.

Whether we failed or passed the test,
I know that we both did our best.
And so these tears, I weep for me;
I do not weep these tears for thee.

Aunt Pazzie

A virtuous woman,
You truly lived a virtuous life,
Your only husband, Jesus Christ.
You dedicated your life to God.
Your services now he will reward.
So peacefully rest now, his love,
For you are destined for above.
You suffered hardship and pain here.
Now he is whispering, "Have no fears."
God knows the struggles you've endured,
And he is here to reassure.
God is just in every way.
"Well done, my servant," he will say.
Your brothers and sisters went on ahead:
Roman, Willie Dora, Ruben, Chester, Monroe, and Ed.
You bore the brunt of love and loss.
You were the last; you paid the cost.
Yet little you had, you gave so much—
Your gift of love, your loving touch.
A sincere tribute to who you are,
A saint of God's, to us a star.

A Beautiful Man

For love I thought I was too old
And that the world was much too cold.
Content within, I tried to be.
Alone, there was no one for me.
Life and love had let me down,
And I looked on it with a frown.
I don't know why, but then one day
Got on my knees and thought to pray.
I asked the Lord to send someone
But did not know that you would come.
From the moment I shook your hand,
I felt closeness I didn't understand.
You touched my spirit and my mind.

Humble and pleasant, one of a kind,
I felt I loved you from the start
And quickly surrendered to you my heart.
You are the answer to my prayer.
My life, my love, I want to share.
When I look deep into your eyes,
So much passion I can't hide.
You fill my list and fantasy.
A beautiful man you are to me.
I fear that I am too deep for you,
And you're not sure just what to do.
It's my desire that you will stay,
But if you must, then back away.
If you and I are meant to be,
God willing, you'll come back to me.

Mama, Your Labor

Mama, your labor was not in vain.
Though we rebelled and caused you pain,
We know you loved us all the same.
We made our choices; you're not to blame.
But returned to Christ from whence we came.
You and Daddy put in the right stuff.
We knew where to turn when things got rough.
God's word that you instilled in us.
He, our refuge in him, we trust.
Of course we had differences and disagreed.
We didn't always see what the other could see,
Mother and daughter at odds sometimes.
But better a friend could not be found.
No, Mama, your labor was not in vain.
We are now parents and know your pain.
We understand and love them the same.
So thank you, Mama, for seeing us through.
Without you, we wouldn't know what to do.
You were chosen to give us life,
Born then reborn in Jesus Christ.

Last Night

Last night, you touched my face.
I reached for you, but you weren't there.
In my mind, you held me close.
I whispered sweet things in your ear.
My love was alone, and I longed for thee.
It was only a fantasy.

Last night, I needed you.
There was nothing you could do.
Last night, I felt a pain
Deep in my psyche I couldn't explain.
Could it be a transformation,
Or just the usual complications?

Last night, I wanted you
To reach for me and pull me close.
You didn't budge, and I didn't dare.
I started to fear you do not care.
Last night, I tried to hide
From all the things I feel inside.
My love was lone and all alone.
I dared not call you on the phone.

Last night seemed to go on and on.

Alive

He walked along the paved road, kicking rocks along the way,

A young boy, full of mischief and play.

His zest for living gave life to me.

Could it be his own demise, the call to be free?

Why him? Why so young? For what purpose could it be?

Maybe for others still alive.

Was it for them to see he died?

That though they are young, there is that possibility?

For him, this was destiny and sad, but yet it was meant to be.

Perhaps when he died,

In Christ then he smiled

Because he was free,

No longer deprived of basic needs.

His purpose was complete.

Am I?

Am I the woman that you see,
On every woman's face you meet
When you're walking down the street,
Are you searching just for me?
If I offer you my heart,
Love you tenderly to start,
Will you break it all in parts
Or discard as damaged art?
Can you love me, heart and soul?
Commit your all to have and hold?
Am I not the one you want?
Honestly, tell me if you don't.